Dear Readers,

This is the story of Garrett Morgan. As a boy, he was very curious. He was always wanting to know how things worked, and why, and how he could make them better.

When Garrett grew up, his curiosity and his desire to improve things led to very useful inventions—inventions that saved lives.

Garrett's main thought in inventing was to help others. How important this thought is!

Your friend,

Garnet Jackson

Garrett Morgan

Inventor

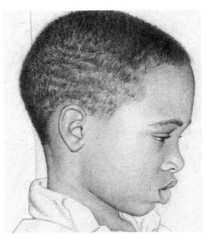

Written by Garnet Nelson Jackson

Illustrated by Thomas Hudson

MODERN CURRICULUM PRESS

Program Reviewers

Maureen Besst, Teacher
Orange County Public Schools
Orlando, Florida

Carol Brown, Director of Reading
Coordinator
Freeport Schools
Freeport, New York

Kanani Choy, Principal
Clarendon Alternative School
San Francisco, California

Barbara Jackson-Nash, Deputy Director
Banneker-Douglass Museum
Annapolis, Maryland

Minesa Taylor, Teacher
Mayfair Elementary School
East Cleveland, Ohio

3 9082 05704898 8

MODERN CURRICULUM PRESS
13900 Prospect Road, Cleveland, Ohio 44136
Simon & Schuster • A Paramount Communications Company

Copyright © 1993 Modern Curriculum Press, Inc.

Library of Congress Catalog Card Number: 92-28801
ISBN 0-8136-5231-6 (Reinforced Binding)   ISBN 0-8136-5704-0 (Paperback)

Text Printed on Recycled Paper

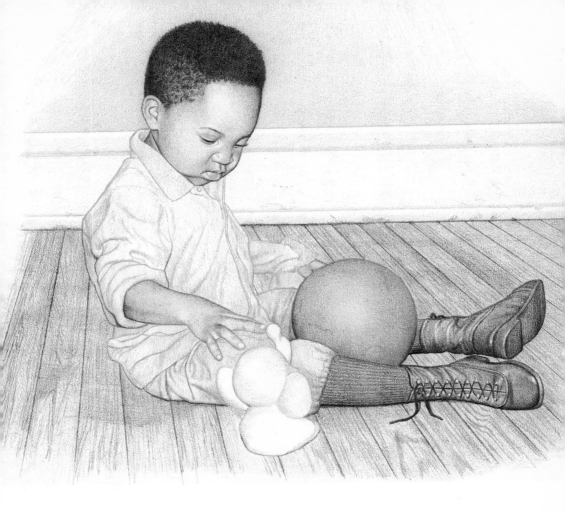

Little Garrett was born
In a small town in Kentucky.
Soon his parents knew
Indeed they were quite lucky.

2

His ten brothers and sisters
Were always around,
But a quiet place for thinking
Garrett often found.

"What?"
"How?"
"Why?"
Were questions he liked to ask.
How to improve a thing
Was his favorite task.

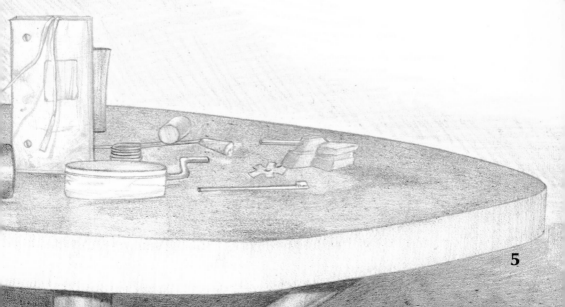

At fourteen years of age
Garrett left his family
And went to Ohio
To see what he could see.

Soon Garrett moved to Cleveland
As his ideas grew.
He opened a repair shop
And began inventing, too.

To provide firefighters
With air that was good,
Garrett invented
The safety hood.

At this time in our country,
On busy streets and roads,
The drivers did not know
Just when to stop or go.

13

14

Garrett saw so many accidents!
So he stated with a frown,
"We must do something different
With the traffic in our towns."

He went into his workshop
And tried a thing or two,
And pretty soon he figured out
What he had to do.

Garrett's great idea
Deserves the highest praise.
He thought of traffic signals
For cars going different ways.

The cars going one way
Must stop for red.
The other cars see green
And move ahead.

Now there's much less confusion
In our streets and towns—
It was 1923
When the solution was found.

22

Red means stop,
Green means go,
Because Garrett Morgan
Told us so.

Glossary

accident (ak´ sə dənt) An unwanted happening that causes someone or something to be hurt

confusion (kən fyo͞o´ zhən) Disorder

deserve (di zʉrv´) To have a right to

invent (in vent´) To think out or make something that had never been made before

signal (sig´ n'l) Something used as a warning or direction

solution (sə lo͞o´ shən) An answer to a problem

traffic (traf´ ik) The movement of cars, people, and so on along a road or pathway

About the Author

Garnet Jackson is an elementary teacher in Flint, Michigan, with a deep concern for developing a positive self-image in young African American students. After an unsuccessful search for materials about famous African Americans written on the level of early readers, Ms. Jackson filled the gap by producing a series of biographies herself. In addition to being a teacher, Ms. Jackson is a poet and a newspaper columnist. She has one son, Damon. She dedicates this book to the memory of her dear mother, Carrie Sherman.

About the Illustrator

Thomas Hudson, a graduate of Cooper School of Art, has worked as a commercial illustrator for eight years. His illustrations have appeared in *Success Guide*, *Renaissance* and *Club Date* magazines. In *Garrett Morgan*, Mr. Hudson uses colored pencils to enrich the text by creating especially vivid illustrations that express the intricate details of the early twentieth century.